WASHITA

Washita

PATRICK LANE

HARBOUR PUBLISHING
www.harbourpublishing.com

2014

Harbour Publishing Co. Ltd.
P.O. Box 219, Madeira Park, BC, V0N 2H0
www.harbourpublishing.com

Cover photograph by Frank I. Reiter
Edited by Elaine Park
Cover and text design by Carleton Wilson
Printed and bound in Canada

Canada Council   Conseil des Arts
for the Arts   du Canada

BRITISH COLUMBIA
ARTS COUNCIL
An agency of the Province of British Columbia

Harbour Publishing Co. Ltd. acknowledges financial support from the
Government of Canada through the Canada Book Fund and the Canada Council
for the Arts, and from the Province of British Columbia through the BC Arts
Council and the Book Publishing Tax Credit.

Cataloguing information available from Library and Archives Canada
ISBN 978-1-55017-676-6 (paper)
ISBN 978-1-55017-677-3 (ebook)

MIX
Paper from
responsible sources
FSC
www.fsc.org   FSC® C107923

This book is for Lorna

as always

"a boy in autumn playing upon an oat-stem flute"

CONTENTS

ARROYO

The dead do not come riding dark horses up out of the arroyo.
They do not arrive in dust, grey-shrouded, singing the old songs.
No, they arrive like turnips pulled winter-burned and cold from the soil.
They lie at your feet, worm-riddled, creased with dirt in the furrows,
fallen peasants left behind in the caterpillar treads of tanks.
And the rags left on the dump by Mandelstam, the holes in the snow by the aspens.
You kneel by the turnips and plead forgiveness; beg the cold winds abate,
that the green world come back, that every seed left dying come again to life.
The stories they told you as a child are rocks in your skull.
That tiny girl in the winter ditch weeping as the logging trucks rolled by.
Her dress was pale as her mother's eyes.
You lie in the long unwinding, wet with worm casts, your tongue burned by salt.
It will take more years than you remember to warm her small hands.

A man should not dream of the frilled skirts of the hooves of horses.
An apple should not be eaten with the burned shadow of a leaf in its flesh.
A woman should bury her man's nail clippings under the dark moon.
There should be no trail to that place, no trail to the fragments of his hair, his spittle.
A mole's tooth, a cat's tail, the heart of a dog, the eye of a frog.
Bring none of these as gifts to the year's first lamb.
A man should not be witness to his daughter's birth or dress his mother's corpse
(This last the teaching of the Greeks on Ios).
A man should burn the branches of the weeping willow. Should he,
Then his sons will have sons, his daughters ovens.
A mother says you should leave your footprint in the dust of her grave
So the wind will remember her. But that mother is dead now.
And the wind forgets and forgets without mercy her passing.

—After Czeslaw Milosz's poem, "Should, Should Not"

ASSINIBOINE

Deep summer nights and you, far off, quiet in the dawn.
That last morning the mute swans were on the river and I was unclean.
I placed hot stones in water as you told me of the old people
beside the slow current singing. If I look hard enough I believe
I can see the swans slide past on that long river going toward the lake.
It took many stones, you weaving grouse feathers in your hair, and laughing.
Do you remember the swans? The birds whose wings were song?
Your mother told you they were ghost birds. *But she was crazy*, you said.
And then the city and you lost again in the bars, the empty rooms.
It was the time one of my last lives was changing.
I looked hard, but there was no finding you.
I turned all the way around then and headed west toward the grey rain.
It was a far way, that walking to the place where the sun drowns.

BARRANQUILLA

There were days he stared at himself in wonder.
His body on the floor, the vodka dribbling from his mouth.
The geraniums in the toilet bowl.
That bar in Barranquilla years ago, the man with the thin blade leaving.
Or the half-blind boy—practicing being
a man in front of his mother's mirror.
1951.
A paring knife in his small hand: *fuck you, fuck you!*
Wanting what he is, not what he was.
The *compadres* in the bar moved away, not wanting to be a part of it.
Vete a la mierda, hijo de puta!
Hate is beautiful in Spanish.
Contempt too, the woman at the table counting the money.
Even now he is unsure if any of it is true.
But there was the outline of a snake carved into that pine headboard:
Hermoso, sí.
Shadows mostly, chimera, ghosts.

BOKUSEKI

Iris blades cut through the last ice on the pond.
Emblems of endurance, they are what a man knows
who asks of the grey clouds they witness his passing.
I don't know where the water goes, remember the thin creek
I drank from when I lived in that cabin by the sea.
The doe grazed among fallen apples in my yard.
When I shot her she hung for a moment in the sky.
There were days back then I lived without regard for life.
Forgiveness comes hard.
Each year I rake the leaves and burn
the winged seeds of maples in the flames.
I kneel by the pond and ask where I am going,
what it is I must do. Bokuseki, these iris blades in ice.
When the rain dries on my palms it leaves the trace of Gobi dust.
Each night I breathe a far desert, vestiges of the fall.

BONSAI

Ts'ze, you love the sheep. I love the ceremony.

—*The Analects of Confucius*, Book III, Chapter XVII

The jay screams his morning song in the derelict pine
as I trim the stump of the old cherry tree.
Even with gloves my hands remember the cold,
remember breaking these wrists when I was a boy.
My arms mended wrong.
On the weathered board by the pond, five bonsai,
their leaves red as spilled blood.
Autumn maples grown from feathered seeds.
Bonsai.
How carefully I torment them every fall, cutting back their limbs and roots.
My chainsaw lies among the scattered rounds of the cherry tree.
Among my fingers, torn ribbons of wind.
In the pond the winter fish consume themselves slowly. Waiting.
So too the night.
Water has its way under the ice.
The jay laughs as he torments the day. And I say, *Never mind*.

BOXWOOD

The child splitting kindling in the cold shed at dawn
is learning how to trust the eye, not the hand,
and not the hatchet, for these last go where the eye wills.
Still, the child will cut himself more than once
until he learns to go past the eye, the kindling falling
like music, sprung notes clear in the morning.

BYA JHATOR

> "I want to believe in one place," he said. "I want it in my blood."
> —Olen Steinhauer, *The Bridge of Sighs*

Three vultures in the ditch below Hartland dump.
A doe lifts her head from the gravel.
Bright dawn and images, this false world.
A vulture takes a hop, a loop of gut in its beak.
Why now, this song of tired messengers?
The doe's eyes, curious, ask nothing of me.
Hers is a modesty I can't touch.
The earth is everywhere and scant.
Infinitesimal creatures rise up to prey on us from the offal we wade in.
As the vulture, we piss on our naked legs and hiss.
I give, as always, alms to the birds, a sky burial, a breath in flight.
The volt hulks on the bare branches of the dead fir.
It is one place, rock, not stone.

It was before the plum blossoms. Before that.
Before the mist and the wind rising from the sea.
And the little brown bats in the false dawn gorging on fragrant moths.
The feast that is the promise of light.
The raccoon was only a tail, a slip in the failing shadow.
And Basho coming home, his ear torn, happy with the night.
And, please, before I forget.
Write this.
Write this down:
the old rat turns and turns in his paws a delicate seed.
And the Horned owl meditates upon death on the yard pole.
O, and yes, before the pilgrim sea lion's moon song
was your hand in my hand in the dark.

Snow dust in the pines and the shadows of swans on skim ice.
The surface breaks and sweet water swims in their feathers.
What joy to sing a last song to the moon.
Twilight is upon me. My poor eyes gather in the dusk.
Surely the earth trembles at the hummingbird's heart in the egg.
The beating knot at the end of a sentence. Large as that.
Among spiderwebs and moss a life will cry come spring.
The Chinese called their Gobi dead *red dust*.
What shall I call you?
Tonight I took my shorn hair and laid it on the arms of the pines.
In the morning the hummingbirds will line their nests with me.

COWICHAN VALLEY POEM

The heron has only one leg
and he stands on both of them.

DISPENSATION

I see the dragonfly and the lily through a grey veil.
The clarity is like what I would like to remember
fine wine is and can't because the distance is too great.
But the accuracy is there in spite of the refusal.
Yesterday I went to the garden as my mother did
in the surety of solitude, my crawling into the dark
in search of skeleton weed and hawkweed,
ragwort, spurge, hound's tongue, toadflax.
The barren earth is what I want, the coolness there.
I know I almost know.
I am by the yellow lilies at the pond
staring at the water through the fretful wing of a dragonfly.
What is this divinity that I must search for it again?
My mother kneels under the mimosa, demure.
Which she wasn't. But that I see her so
through the dragonfly's pellucid wing. Going blind slowly.
The deep beyond the gossamer. The purity of that.

The wooden ladle is thin, worn away by stone.
I cup my hands in the basin, lift water to my mouth.
The high creeks find their way to quiet waters.
I was at home on the gravel bars until poetry drew me away to the city.
I fished the high lakes with my brother, dead now these many years.
An old man found the ladle in the back of his shop in Fan Tan Alley.
A wooden spoon carved in a village northwest of far Xian.
Strange, the sudden memory of a spoon I carved as a boy.
A child of the bush, I wanted to be alive in a simpler time.
It is foolish of me now to look at my hands and remember
how difficult it was to carve the ladle's bowl with a knife blade.
I think of that spoon now, the wind drying my hands.
How far away a poem can take you from the world.
The quail bring their young to the stone basin at dawn.
One and by one they lift their heads, cool water running down their throats.

EARLY PROMISES

The blue just before blue, dawn, the hard shade that promises
nothing, an old knife tempered wrong in tired coals,
the blacksmith drunk and weeping in the bar, the horses gone.
You watch the woman with the canvas coat,
the one who gathers bottles from the blue boxes tilted on the curb.
She knows the answers, but she's not telling anyone.
It's a wrong time to be awake and you don't yearn for the bed
you didn't have in the night, the girl who left you in that bar years ago.
The pool table lights turned her blonde hair blue, shadows
that lived no longer than the moment you touched them.
You wonder sometimes about the girl but she's gone into the bruised lands.
Coming out of the night is harder than you think.
You walk blind into morning thinking of a tongue on glass, the moon.

ELI, ELI

The quail in the garden eat the fallen sunflower seeds.
Terrible and sweet, the beauty in this world,
as the prayer I made in childhood: *Eli, Eli,*
save my father in the war.
My greed for simple things is endless.
The dry hills above Naples have little to do with me,
and the shallow streams running blue above Rouen
where the children play among the apple trees, screaming.
The elusive voices of the last century sing to me of who I was.
The old man carved a quail from ivory to hang from his obi.
Netsuke.
The living birds bathe in the dust by the dying asters.
I am almost afraid to put them in this poem.

FOR THE WOMAN WHO DANCED
WITH THE ASHES OF HER SON

Strange how beautiful when we are diaphanous,
a bit of ripped muslin set against the sun, the wind
soft as a child's skin. Tragedy does that to us
and we are made the greater for our smallness.
A bright pebble among the discarded shells.
There are times I am a questing mole, fierce
in my love, lost as anything alive.

HARD-ROCK

My father's chest hid his songs in the crannies.
His lungs created elaborate cathedrals from quartz dust,
a crystal symphony playing Mahler under water.
Scar tissue, the kind without nerves, which he was without,
walking always into the far reaches of the mine.
My mother told me he was silent in those days.
On a slant shadow at the mine mouth, a lynx spider rests;
difficult air, old bones, and dust under the skree.
The creature rests on nervous grass, hinged on crushed rock,
wandering cat, wilder of gullies and ravines.
My father sat much alone by the falls below the cabin.
He told me once he lived inside the crash of water on stones.
I lie beside the spider, wrists crossed, my many eyes closed.
A cellist told me once such presence is where the god waits to eat us.

HIRAGANA

In the slanted light from the window, the moon tonight cut in half.
Tonight I am a cursive fragment, a poor master.
My dead mother sent me from her knees.
She listened to the radio for word of the invasion.
Left alone, there was no place safe from my pillaging.
I address her here, humbly, with too many words, say:
the stumps from the old time are nurseries now.
They are all that is left of the great slaughter.
Swordferns and cedars shade them to their rest.
On the beach pebbles shine in the rain.
This world is best seen from the knees.
Everything is narrow now, a secular path.
I wish I could bring home the deities, but
there are only a white stone and a red stone to worship today.
I bow down in the rain, modest, a brush stroke only.

HUNGER

The doe, her fawn torn apart by dogs,
mews as a kitten does. Bewildered, she turns
her one brown eye toward the hills, and slow,
hoof by small hoof, moves tentative away.
The sounds behind her are the dogs' wet cries.
A thinness among the yelps, and her then stopping
to smell the new grass by a stone. Head down,
a single shiver across her lean rump, a fly
at rest there riding her quiet from the meadow.

IKI

And maybe it isn't beauty he wants. Maybe he wants
the feral dog draped in the ditch below Hartland dump
to be a fur stole fallen from a bare shoulder and forgotten,
a slim woman moving from the piano, every eye upon her
in the Empress Theatre of sixty years ago. It's a long way
from Bette Davis to the vultures folding their wings
in the oldest geier the world knows, their hunger spiral.
Tearer, purifier. Or is affliction nearer to the truth of things?
Are the birds that lumber awkwardly a pantomime
as they lean to the flesh? Is *All About Eve* all about Eve?
Bette Davis lived in my father's eyes. My mother in the early photos
wore the face and shoulders of a concubine, hard and cold and without pity.

IMAGO

We come from the sea of our mother's salt blood,
hang upside down from our father's hands and weep.
And what of the birds singing in the laurel,
the brittle leaves enough to keep the cat at bay?
Where does the butterfly sleep whose wings are glory?
What wish has the fox who grins among the tall grasses,
the bear dancing in the stream?
Something tries to go dead in us all the time
even as deep in the earth the cicada dreams its imago.

INFORMIS

In the gully an Indian boy plunged his hand into an ant mound for a dollar.
I stood aside as the men from the highway crew watched his flesh
become another thing, a red swarm screaming.
Some days our bones shine through our skin,
but such times are bitter music, their history best lost.
We take away everything we can to keep the mystery intact.
It is why in the morning I turn the porridge down to seethe.
The woman who moved with me from motel to motel worked hard at her unhappiness.
She told me it was all she could do not to place her face in the steam.
There is a flawed beauty in that other world.
You could spend a whole life trying to find the portal close at hand.
The boy, the ants, and little shade on that stretch of highway north of Cache Creek.
If you want a metaphor I could say she was a pine tree without a shadow.
She was the quiet of the ewe in the paddock
dying of the dead lambs inside her,
grazing anyway at the scant desert grass after a night's rare rain,
the cactus gone mad in sudden glory blooming.

IN SNOW WHEN CREATURES AWAKEN
TO SUCH BEAUTY

In the night tunnels, in the fallen grass laid waste by winter,
a creature small and questing finds its way
in the dark woven galleries of the dead.
Kneeling in the drifts I see it pass below me
in the labyrinthine galleries of snow.
Once in ice I saw a fly dance as if in amber,
a dark flaw caught by the moon, an infracted blaze,
a wound made in some alien Baltic age, a violation
beautiful as a shadow moving in the underworld,
this winter, impossible and amazed.

INCOHERENCE

He squats in the sun, the koi breaching in the pond.
Their golden backs break the waters. If he reaches out
he can touch them a moment before they flee, a moment to return,
mouths gaping as he thinks men drowning under ice must gape,
their hunger for a sky gone cold.
He knows the way out, but persists as Persephone did,
promising the dead they will have the chance to die again.
Far from the north the snowy owl waits on the fence by the airport.
She starves perfectly.
Inside her feathers there is nothing left but bones.

INNOCENCE

Delivered a baby girl one time in the North, a little one
wet with her mother's blood, the caul a veil.
The baby wept when first she breathed the world.
Secrets then were kept in silence, the young ones hidden away.
The mother signed to me, mute girl, as her father raged.
I tried to understand her hands, not knowing the sign for love.
Three days later their battered trailer swung wide
over the brown waters below Mad River bridge.
Salmon red as tears swarmed among the dead in the shallows.
A woman I know spoke to me once of the violence in my life.
Your poems are the disfigurement of innocence, she said.
I told her the mist above the river hid the mountains,
that I tried not to think
when I washed her blood away in the creek without a name.

LICHEN WHITE

Lichen white, she lies in a narrow bed,
light among the icons and the glyphs.
The coffin is small that homes a child to rest.
Who placed her there bears her without weight.
Still, he staggers as he weaves among the stones,
his shoulders pale as a gossamer web at dawn.
A chill surrounds him, down from the Monashee,
the lines of the hills a wrong blue, the dry leaves breaking.
A hard earth waits for a poor man's shovel.
Who buries his child walks now without bones,
his flesh white as bled snow.

LIMBO

The red truck by the barn, rust on its fenders.
Ice crystals grew there like forgotten cities,
the windshield a broken star where a face found itself shining.
Close your eyes. There are only the old answers.
The antelope calf lay curled in snow, her black hooves crossed,
her head blunt as the axe my father used to break dry willow.
There are hearts that give off heat days after they stop beating.
A scuff of snow where she stumbled in the cold.
The North held me long before it let me go.
There are these fragments: the little graves outside the cemetery fence past Rosetown.
They buried the babies beyond the wire in limbo.
Plastic flowers in the snow.
There is a great fear in the world.
Jesus, sweet Jesus, I know you're not coming back.
My mother told me there are children so fragile they exist only as angels.
I swear it upon her eyes, those dark knots of blue.

A cougar drank at my creek, the two of us one thought.
And the chocolate lily on the talus slope on the mountain.
A frail beauty in the wind come off the snow.
My hands pick cottonwood leaves from where the birds come to bathe.
I try to remember:
my brother's last words, my father falling, a bullet in his heart.
Listen. I am a cup dropped on stone.
I lean forward because I almost have it and don't.
Do you know the wild horse poem?
The sound of unshod hooves on desert grass, running?

LITTLE HELL'S GATE

Tonight I will dream the old darkness, content.
I say *blue* and my teenage wife weeps over the kitten my father killed.
I remember the petals of her blue dress around her thin legs, kneeling.
The ice gives way at Little Hell's Gate.
Thunder on the river.
How the world dies and dies when we are torn.
There is nothing sweeter than loss.
Such blessed imperfections.
A girl on her knees holds a dead kitten.
What break in us are rivers, the ice going out.

MEDITATION IN THE BAY OF OTTERS

The singing at night among the cedars after the drums,
in the dark as all such voices are and so of loneliness and not
the scream of the heron at dusk: not that misery.
A wrenched solitude, like skin at dawn among the stones.
The smell of burnt sawdust after rain, the chains in the mill quiet at last.
You pause as the words veer down a narrow tunnel and you write:
there was the woman who bared her breasts when you were twelve,
delivering the paper to her each winter morning, her lost gesture,
and now sixty years later trying to understand the contradictions of loneliness.
The cup of thick cocoa, hot and steaming, she had made for you.
You set the cup down carefully on the pine table, pale steam rising.
I'm sorry, you said, your voice not yet broken, the changes still to come.
Ah, but she is far away and surely dead,
or nodding in some ward where men can't hurt her anymore.
Burnt sawdust is how you remember it, thin smoke, the unsteady wind,
the drums still down the shore, and a woman in the utter dark.

MERLIN

All else rage, for my breath stopped at her cry,
her spirit flown as one to the throne of otherness,
where some god she alone knew needed her to die.

The day comes crying like wet silk, slow,
the burden of morning an old capacity resembling love.
Oh, the decades keep me shining.
I touch the broken words, the forms:
clouds in the dawn, pale surprises.
Blessings vanish, the snow falls fast.
This is the ordinary light, a past so far back
I can't find the beginning in all its war and poverty.
Death's symmetry fills me with shells and skulls.
Solitude, that simple anchoritic dance is not enough.
I am lost in an imagined cemetery.
I have brought out my dead.
They stagger down the beach, a spare snow spilling from their eyes.

MUJO

You try to remember the last time you touched her.
You look at hares coupling, the pureness of that,
the buck falling away insensible,
and the wail of the doe just before she licks herself.
Or the eye of the hawk who died in your hands,
somewhere her eggs cold among sticks and bark,
the thrush who tried to lift his dead mate from the road.
There is no word for the skin high up the inner thigh,
for what lies beneath the lobe, the under wrist
where veins and tendons grow in fragile sprawl.
You say her skin was another texture, ice petals,
her bones white willows moving inside snow,
but that is like dragging a grey wing across cement.
You lie in the dark, your cheeks dry.
You know what her skin was, draped thin over bone.
But there is no telling anyone. A thrush maybe, a hare,
or a meadowhawk, that thin creature arranged on glass.

MUTE SWANS

And the departures: the mute swans flying out of the dawn,
their pale wings against the moon and the false light broken.
There are thin waves on the gravel, on the broken shells.
Drums begin down the shore, the first people singing in the longhouse.
I tell you I could fly when I was a child.
I swear it on the clouds that carried me to the sea.
But that time too is gone.
The wind drives the white spirits into the trees.
The stars swarm in terrible fires, in endless ice.
There are no stories, but that I make them so.
I am on my knees now translating the wedged language of the swans,
the obsolete informing of their shadows on the snow.

The blade found its way in the wood, my young body
bringing the splitting axe down, the weight breaking
the rounds of fir. A kind of longing, the groan of old wood,
the fallen tree remembering its childhood below the cliff
a hundred years ago, and winter hard around me.
Each season has its song, the chainsaw's scream, the wedge
under the sledge, breaking through the knots
where the limbs once grew, the hardness hidden
in the heart. Ah, long ago, the thin light from the shed
burning the snow, the split wood piling up around me,
my young wife at the window folding diapers, her hot tears
on the worn cotton, a child weeping, and the arc of
the swing, my blade a bright star burying itself in wood.

The whales and ships on the killing grounds off Valparaíso.
The sails drawn and the whales at rest under the full moon,
the waters turned by blood to rust in the pale light.
Flayed bodies slide from the ships. The whales nose the carcasses,
blunt heads still fleshed, the fat there thin and of no use.
And the fires burn, the fat renders, the men circle the vats.
How else but by the flensing knives huge as paddles,
the blocks straining, at times a whale still breathing,
its skin lifted away in strips, the sighs, huge and unimaginable.
And my staring in the night at the slaughter, awake in the dark
with a sorrow so great I wish to be dead that it torment me no more:
the whales in the moonlight at rest after the long pursuit,
the calves sinking to nurse in the deep, rising alone into their mothers' blood.
I see them in the light as if from the moon's height, flying,
as much gull as man, my shaman close to my wings.
She tells me my tears are made from the ocean's blood, old and old,
and far, and far away the whales at sleepless rest, the day's new hunt to come.
I watch the fires, the ships, the men worn thin as they labour at their largesse,
the sea a loneliness as lost as their shouts, the three-year voyage done,
their dream of the bars at the foot of the funiculars where the whores wait,
my sleep sundered, broken by the whales and the ships off Valparaiso.

PARTITA IN A MINOR

A flute perhaps, its virtue to be alone with the small bells in the pines.
Lily stalks reflected in the framed glass of a picture of lily stalks.
The mind moves much as a starving goat moves in a forgotten paddock.
Desiccated leaves, the wind with its fine, clear rattle.
And a woman in her kitchen dances with the ashes of her dead son.
The privilege of despair, how it gathers her in as an oboe gathers the dawn.
I imagine her steps as the kind I used to take among the rattlesnakes.
The steps were simple and of a kind only the bereft ones know.
I was so young then, practising what I would later know as love.
Did I tell you to bring your flute when you come?
Her bare feet on the tiles are the sound of brushes on old drums.

I could wish poems happened more, but wanting them
only leads to the impediment of desire and desire
is never equal to the act. It's much the same as looking back,
expecting a story and finding the characters already dead.
The surprise of that. How the past gets worn down by idle use.
These days the poem comes much as the first bat does
in the false dawn, its flight the mental stumble that I love.
I have my hungers even as they elude me.
Things are so simple, a bat, and the consequent moth
I create to keep my world whole a little longer.
The poems come to me now as occasions, the good ones rarely.
The moth, its wings so white they startle me, escapes.
For the moment. I watch the violence of the dance,
the bat, and the moth too, veering.

QU'APPELLE HILLS

A child dances in the hills to a bone flute.
He is the sound of antelopes breathing.
Behind his eyes are many years of dust.
Come and listen. He is here only for you.

I woke up on Six Mile Creek, a willow grouse falling from the sky.
I baked her, wrapped in clay, in the coals of a long fire,
wisps in the pines, the smoke waiting for the moon.
My brother had fished the pools all day and come back empty.
He sat by the fire stones, lying about the rainbow that got away,
a blanket wrapped around thin shoulders, damp coals in his eyes.
The good days and nights before his death, before it all ended.
I was trying then to live a life without artifice.
That I failed did not diminish my reverence for things.
Those many weeks I disappeared into the blue bush country.
I offered my brother the breast meat, a chunk of fry bread.
He took them gladly, telling me how he was going to run away to the city. Again.
His wife and kids scraped by on welfare, cold nights and withered glass, waiting.
I look out the window at the day coming on, grey clouds without end.
Some mornings the maple leaves fall and my heart has no dignity.
Some mornings there's just too much rain.

RYOANJI

The path narrow at the corner and the old monk on his knees
gathering pine needles in a willow basket, dew on the moss,
the trace of the nun's small shoes among the stones.
She led me at first light past her meditation by the pond.
When I was young I built a pool in the thin creek by my door.
This morning I meet again the cougar at dawn,
my hands cupped, water slipping like years through my fingers.
The mountain had no name, the creek as well.
We arrive as water does with no identity beyond light.
It is rare to see the dew gathering itself on bamboo leaves.
The turtles lie deep among the roots of the water lilies.
A chickadee sips a drop of water from a pine needle
and the nun lives in me still in the quiet I glimpsed, the heron by the pond,
so many years ago now, her thin hand guiding me on the path,
far from home, the poem not written until now.

SABI

A pheasant rises wild from the pea vines.
A shadow settles in the maze of poverty grass.
Home at last, I scrub my hands, the peasant's song in me.
Things move through things. My son's first hands in air.
Each time I see the crescent moon I see his small head crowning.
The past declines.
A pale cloth hangs between me and the sun.
Years ago my mother strained blueberries through white muslin.
I wore it over my childish face, a thin ghost laughing.
Stained shroud, my skin streaked with berry blood.
In the desert lichens eat my father's stone at the speed of stars.
We are of this world and no other.
Crude and rough, my old eyes searching among the weeds.

SANCTUARY

I try to find *sanctuary* in the labyrinth of my mind.
The word eludes me, ill lit in a dark tunnel of bone.
My father's headlamp hisses deep in the hard-rock mine.
A child, I laid my head on his chest to hear the crystals sing.
One search leads to another: my mother in the lamplight.
The centuries are small as the pins in her sewing cushion.
I took them out and pushed them slowly through my skin,
my wrist bones fragile as a little clock.
The drops grew like rubies, and once an artery, the blood a tiny fountain.
Refuge, asylum.
Which of the many seeds in my father's body was I?
I see the thousands of my dead brothers and sisters swarming.
The chancel of her womb. Misplaced words, lost souls.
When I am at last blind I will see her, clearly.
1914.
1939.
She will tell me again we are harbingers of death.

SCARIFY

The welts he gave to his body when he wanted
to feel something, his flesh rising white to the whip
he made from the laces in his father's boots.
In the old books from the Empire, children
wore on their faces designs beyond their skin.
The girl's wounds were pearls dribbled on her flesh.
He dreamed her necklace scars on his tongue.
I watch the old turtle dry her shell in the sun.
Within her is the patience of old blood.
In the lee of a dune a child rubs dust into a wound.
This is my body, the boy says, touching the scar on his chest.
O Lord, I knew that boy.
Let someone hold him close.

SCREE

The broken stones are mountains in the ruts by the desert gate. Even so, the ant does not hesitate as it drags the butterfly over the high passes.

SHELTER

My friend before he died looked only to the wind.
Near the end he lay down on straw in a rough-hewn house, the clutter gone.
In the ditch black ants scurry among the bright feathers of a dying quail.
They feast on the eggs of fleas, the unborn unable to shun the body.
It was west of Moose Jaw where the rolling hills began. I remember now:
white wood, pale sky, the shells of bark dry cups where the grass slept.
The old barn in the shelterbelt was trying to lie down.

Her silk stocking, the thin dress breathing as ash does when it falls.
Salt on his tongue, the strand of hair wet below the lobe.
The unheard, the ear of the sleeping cat turned toward quiet with intent.
Three boots on the narrow shelf, the severed legs in the bin after.
The bone man picking lice from the seams of his cap,
a dry rain, the kind they call *tears of dust* in Blida,
the refusal of despair even as the carrion crow calls the names.
Those last nights, Camus writing: *l'absence totale d'espoir.*
And the ninth bell in Hoko-ji, the one they let rest for fifty years,
the bronze needing to learn sound before the carved log could strike it.
As the emptiness poor men leave of their bodies in the ash of the beehive burner,
the care they take at dawn to follow each inward step out so none will wake.
Without wind, the gesture, as of a woman wanting to be seen, not easily, but well.

At seventy I followed my heart ... the withered vines on the lattice
shiver in the rain. That old man knew a thing or two about things.
I am trying hard not to depend on letters. Throw this into the flames
when you're done. I read Confucius when I was young
and couldn't wait to get old. Green sticks bend easily in the wind.
Sew, seam, suture, sutra, everything connects, a thread leading us on.
It may be that the Minotaur was the silence at the end of a song.
The young poets give up form before they've got it. They want to mean a thing.
How sanctity gets lost in a scattering of straw. The germ is in the seed,
saved for the season to come, the ritual of the virgin burying the grains in spring,
a boy in autumn playing upon an oat-stem flute. Withered vines.
The dry leaves scatter in the wind coming in off the sea.
Amazed, I hang in this dark by a thread, listening.

SOLACE

What am I meant to miss, the long thread the swallows pull
through the water when they drink on their wings?
Is it the rattlesnake in her new skin in the sun, spring on the drifted rocks
where the mountain flares her skirts above the buds of the paintbrush,
the heat fooling the flower into a month of early frosts, too soon?
Or the snake having come up from her winter den where she lay,
her skin still damp, curled like gauze fallen from a wound
around a flake of pine bark, the scant red turned pale
enough to see through? What are my eyes now, kneeling by the bed
in the sun, you sleeping, the flush above your wrist,
the faint hairs worn thin by your golden bracelet,
against your neck a jade earring dangling, closed now, seeing?
Is it the chickadee with a pine seed under its claw
chittering at me from a branch above my head? No,
I am not there. That was years ago.
I am not grieving as I watch the snake,
the first of the long shadows touching her, retreat into the earth
as the swallows slip from the lake, the water quiet, the cutthroats
in the creek mouth feeding in the runoff come down from the hills.

SOLSTICE COMING

Typing with my left forefinger today. The poem is immensely slow,
one letter, one word, one line at a time. This and then this and ...
amazing how the images slow to an intimate crawl,
each word a salamander peering from beneath a stone.
The fish this winter are wraiths, the pond's perfect thoughts.
I have tried to love this quiet as the hours pass through me.
It is rare to feel anything deeply. My life is a feast if I allow it to be.
The slow rain falls without cease. It eats the ice, one drop at a time.
These days my body breaks down and I cannot lift my right arm.
My poems now are thin as I was when I lived in the mountains.
I tried to believe the lake when I came down from the high snows.
I watched the water for a long time from the safety of the trees.
It was a trout rising made me see what a day is, a ripple only.

SUBMISSION

It is not dark, just blurred, distorted by the retina rotting at the centre.
Not yet, he said, sitting on the stage while a stranger read his poems.
In wonder, his struggle in the dark, which it wasn't, not yet.
He thinks of Borges listening to a woman turn the pages
and hears a hunchback in Paris cry out: *Sanctuaire!*
Outside the swans pass against the last of sky.
They sing of a salt marsh in Texas, warm water on their breasts.
You will see the peripheral, the doctor said, the nurse smiling.
Penumbra.
Years ago he watched the moon blot out the sun,
a terrible ring of light,
the bats coming out into the uncertain cold, the new night,
and the blind panic he understands now, in dark submission raging.

SUNYATA

My dead brother casts into the shadow of a pool on Six Mile Creek.
A trout swims to his hook and I drown, thrashing in the air.

SWARF

My father pointed to the redtail on the yard pole.
How beautiful my eyes among imagined feathers.
My first teacher, young and gentle, told me I couldn't see.
That's when the work began, one letter, one word at a time.
The art of diminishing returns: a humble birth and then the dictionary.
I sharpened my father's axe head through years of fallen trees.
Was I the blade or the stone?
Going blind twice: this cup a private beauty, crazed lines.
I sip my tea and stare into the net of things.
Yesterday the sea lions fed on the herring shoal in the bay.
Today gulls worry the corpses.
A mother vomits into the scream of her young.
I began blind. It will end so.
Warp and weft.
I have nothing left to offer but a worn Washita stone,
wood and water in the ceremony of the dark.

As the mouse seems with its bundle of maggots to breathe.
Rice grains among my fingers, tiny mouths suckling as their mothers cry.
The belly is a cleft, the fur a desert, bared teeth, the eyes gone gaping.
As the dead steer I saw as a boy in the blue bush hills.
The stone I dropped into the moil.
What is hell that I am drawn to that torn maw singing?
The flies dreaming in the seethe, their blue bodies heavy with eggs.
What choir keening cleans a world without a need for death?
Those savage songs that call the angels to our rest.
Where the mind goes when there is no way to find the way.
The mouse sits in the cup of my hands.
There is no music sweeter than dark mothers in the night.

He told his wife he lived in the ecstasy of no
and she told him to write that down. The last
he saw was her going into the airport, brightly.
Home, he digs at dawn in the garden, turning
the old earth, giving its buried face to the sun.
Around his neck is the new timer on a cord,
the bread in the stove waiting for its ring.
The noise reminds him he is old, the *tic, tic, tic,*
an ant tap dancing on his chest.
His wife is afraid he will burn the house down.
Some days he wants to burn his new poems.
He thinks he will return to the kitchen, and then
tries to resist when the timer rings.
In this he resembles the aging fighter who tries
to avoid the blows by hanging onto the ropes.
It is a terrible wanting, this being alive.

THE POET, WANTING MORE

/

It means little to me now, this confusion of poets, the everywhere of them.
I think if I walked back into the blue bush country
I would find one of the caves, the ones where I used to sit in the dark, waiting.
It wasn't hiding because there was no one looking for me.
I was waiting. That was it, the hours in the dark.
And then the coming out into the clear light of August
to the blinding. That was the best part, the quick pain in the eyes
and not closing them to what they couldn't see.
It is almost enough not to write anymore, the exceptional being
the ones who watch, the ones who watch, carefully.
If there is a metaphor it would be when I sat among the snakes
in one of the old hibernacula in spring, the thickness of their bodies,
the dense weight in my hands as I held one of the great fathers to my ear
so I could listen to the whisper of his breathing.
Like that, I think.
But it's not like that anymore.

THE UNBEARABLE BEAUTY OF DESPAIR
ALBERT CAMUS WROTE OF IN HIS LAST NIGHTS

The song was of myself and beauty, paradise lost
in the light slipping away from the east window,
the sleep I had fallen into rousing me to wander
into old shadows, the splash of the waterfall by the pond,
the past, the crash of white water on broken stone
in the gorge of Sheep Creek, and the well my father made
so my mother wouldn't have to climb up from the ravine
with the buckets of water she needed to cook, to clean,
to wash her dark hair, our hands, my father's back
as he leaned forward in the tub that sat on the floor
he laid in that cabin just below the Kootenay Bell,
the raw boards he nailed, the walls he raised,
and the windows, their panes of glass scrubbed clean.
I can see my mother's hands lift from the water
to scour the quartz crystals from the curve of his white back,
her wishing she could wash from his lungs the crystals
that were eating him alive, tiny quartz animals
living inside the scars my father grew in his chest
and the bullet that killed him before the silicosis could.
And she was beautiful kneeling beside him
and he was beautiful in his weariness, the water
she carried up from the roaring creek
and, hot from the wood stove, poured over his back.
I was sleeping in the drawer she'd taken out of the bureau
and placed behind the stove to keep me warm
and though this is a story I have imagined again,
one I have told over and over until it has become a song
that has invaded me, the words repeating inside me,
it is the first where I've placed my father
in the corrugated iron washtub and my mother
washing him, her hands on his heavy body,

the whispers of quartz in his lungs, the war still to come,
and the ragged melody I woke into, a vesper sparrow
singing to himself among the laurel leaves at dawn.

TRADITION

They named the trees without asking the trees their names.
The shame of my people is without beginning, without end.
I tell you, the wren cannot be taught good manners,
nor the hummingbird to fly, the robin to listen to the earth.
Under the bridge on the Skeena
baby swallows fall from their nests on ancient wings.
Old boards are stacked upon old boards.
There is no other way. By the glacial river
I walked in the hollowed paw prints a grizzly bear left
ten thousand years ago this morning.

TREADLE

Streams slow in the mind, under the clay banks, pockets of fat trout,
browns and cutthroats in the late spring, their bellies thick.
The smoke in water that is an otter at play.
There was a man carried glass over these mountains on his back.
The clarity of imperfections, ripples only a thumb could feel.
The single pane I found unbroken in a cabin up Lost Line Creek.
Promises get lost. They are like paper scraps wedged in old bark.
How young I was to think I could remember everything:
a rusted old Singer sewing machine under a deserted cabin window.
Oiled paper gave light as if from drenched fire, yellow smoke.
But there are men who will do anything for a woman who wants to see forever.
The light still pours into my eyes through her glass window.
I can see her now watching him come up the trail from the creek.
He is holding a string of trout, browns and cutthroats.
He tells her he left a single fish on the stepping stone for the otter.
In the little sewing machine drawer was the nest of a white-footed mouse.
Her babies were tiny pink thumbs, blind as dreams.

UGUISUBARI

My hand on the winter bamboo.
The leaves are the sound of dry bones clashing under boots.
Walk the old way, every clod of earth holds blood.
Stillness of water, stillness of poetry.
The thief ant floats on its leaf toward paradise.
A shadow leaves its shadow on the earth.
Bamboo on bamboo, a leaf, a thought.
How we are of this world, this portal to yugen.
The cat places his paw on the corpse of a hermit warbler.
He lifts his head and asks me where I am.
Here, I say, *here.*
Yes and no.
The old artisan studied for years to make a nightingale floor.

WAR

My mother held her hand above the kettle boiling on the stove.
The steam surrounded her in the way a mist does
when a grouse flies into it, leaving only the flight song of wings.
My father walked away into the night.
Everything he left was quiet then, my brothers at the table
holding spoons to their red lips, and me
crouched behind the wood stove holding my breath, waiting
for whatever was going to happen,
the kettle screaming, and mother not moving, again.

WARBLER

I hold in my hands her yellow wings.
They are what bamboo leaves offer to the rake.
The tiny knuckles of her claws grip nothing.
They are the hands of my mother on her deathbed.
I place her beside the stupa of the fallen daisy,
cover her with a robe of white petals.
There are restraints and they are without fault.
The spirit leaves us slowly, forever.
It is the waiting I try to understand, the quietness of that.

I prayed for the doe this morning,
the other world come alive again in me, old songs and soft birds.
Like you I have carried the sorrows.
They are as small now as a koan carved on a grain of rice.
This morning I looked into the bronze mirror and found still water,
my face almost young again as I lifted her head,
cut her warm throat under the apple tree,
the blood flowing across my wrist.

GLOSSARY

"*Ars Poetica*"
+ after Czeslaw Milosz's poem, "Should, Should Not"

"Assiniboine"
+ title refers to a river in the southern prairie of Saskatchewan and Manitoba

"Barranquilla"
+ title refers to a city in southwest Colombia
+ *Compadres* (Spanish), companions
+ *Vete a la mierda, hijo de puta* (Spanish), "Eat shit, you sonofabitch"
+ *Hermoso, sí* (Spanish), "Beautiful, yes"

"Bokuseki"
+ title from the Japanese *seki*, traces, and *boku*, ink; early Zen writings

"Bonsai"
+ title from the Japanese *bonsai*, tray planting
+ epigraph from *The Analects of Confucius*, Book iii, Chapter xvii: "Ts'ze-kung wished to do away with the offering of sheep for sacrifice connected with the inauguration of the first day of the month."

"Bya Jhator"
+ title refers to sky burial, a Tibetan funerary practice in which the corpse is left out for vultures
+ "volt" is a collective noun for a gathering of vultures

"Calligraphy"
+ Basho, our cat, is named for Matsuo Basho (1644–94), a great poet of the Edo period in Japan

"Cowichan Valley Poem"
+ dedicated to Richard Osler

"Eli, Eli"
+ *eli* (Hebrew), ascent

"Hiragana"
+ *Hiragana* are feminine brushstrokes in Japanese calligraphy, originally *on'na de*

"Iki"
- *iki* (Japanese), blunt, unwavering directness
- Bette Davis (1908–89), American movie star
- *All About Eve*, 1950 movie drama

"Incoherence"
- Persephone is the goddess of the underworld in Greek mythology

"Innocence"
- "Your poems are the disfigurement of innocence," a remark made by the poet, Sharon Thesen, for which I am grateful

"Limbo"
- in Christian theology, limbo is the abode after death of the souls of unbaptized infants

"Little Hell's Gate"
- title refers to a dog-leg narrowing of the North Thompson River canyon

"Merlin"
- title refers to a small, pugnacious falcon, *Falco columbarius*

"Mujo"
- *mujo* (Japanese), impermanence
- Red-veined meadowhawk, *Sympetrum madidum*, dragonfly

"Off Valparaíso"
- title refers to a port city of Chile

"Partita in A Minor"
- title refers to a piece of music in four movements for solo flute by Johann Sebastian Bach
- dedicated to Martha Royea

"Qu'Appelle Hills"
- title refers to the region of the Qu'Appelle River and valley in southern Saskatchewan. The name is a corruption of a French phrase, *qui appelle?* (who calls?)

"Ryoanji"
- Ryoanji is a dry landscape (*Karesansui*) rock garden created in Kyoto, Japan, during the fifteenth century

"Sabi"

+ *sabi* (Japanese), the beauty and serenity that comes with age

"Scree"

+ title refers to broken rock fragments at the base of mountain crags

"Slack Beauty"

+ title phrase is from the text of an essay by the American poet, Jack Gilbert
+ Blida, a city in Algeria
+ Carrion crow, *Corvus corone*, a native crow of North Africa
+ Albert Camus wrote of *l'absence totale d'espoir* (French), the total absence of hope
+ Hoko-ji, a temple in Kyoto, Japan, containing the *bonsho* bell commissioned by Toyotomi Hideyori, last of a series of nine bells cast in August 1612

"Soft and Moist, Hard and Dry"

+ "At seventy I followed my heart," from *The Analects of Confucius*

"Sunyata"

+ *sunyata* (Japanese), emptiness

"Swarf"

+ swarf is grit from grinding metal or dust from sawing wood
+ the Washita is a sharpening stone fashioned out of white quartz rock from the Ouachita Mountains of Arkansas

"Uguisubari"

+ *uguisubari* (Japanese), the 'nightingale floor' designed to make chirping noises when walked upon to warn inhabitants of anyone approaching
+ *yugen* (Japanese), the depth of the world we live in, subtle, mysterious

"Wishing Not to Be Aloof Like Stone"

+ title is a paraphrase of the last line from Book 1, Section XXXIX, of the *Tao te Ching*

I've been a right-handed, one-finger typist for the fifty-five years of my writing life, many short stories, three failed novels, a memoir, a completed novel, and many books of poetry. It was after the novel, *Red Dog, Red Dog*, was published that I began the second of what I imagined would be a trilogy. One hundred and seventy pages into that next novel my right shoulder froze and I was unable to lift my arm to type. After several crippled weeks I tried to work on a poem. Unable to use my right arm, hand, and forefinger, I used my left, but discovered that the right side of my brain did not know where the lettered keys were. The process of typing became excruciatingly slow, each key having to be searched for visually before I could type a letter and then finish a word. A word such as *The* came very slowly, a *T* and an *h* and then an *e* ... the word, *The*, safely there and then the relief of the space bar. In the time it took to accomplish the typing that simple article I had discarded numerous adjectives and numberless nouns, my mind reeling at the possibilities language offered in the time between letters. The majority of the poems in this collection are the result of that discovery. The process of writing each poem was exquisite, each letter, each word, and each line meditations rare and beautiful. My imagination became an eddy in a meadow creek, a thin trout in turning water. Each letter was a dry fir needle circling above slow brown fins.

In this late time of my life I am in debt to many people. You know who you are. My gratitude to you all. You have blessed my life with your presence. I name here only my companion, Lorna Crozier, wife, lover, and friend. She is my one, my private beauty.

ABOUT THE AUTHOR

Patrick Lane, considered by most writers and critics to be one of Canada's finest poets, was born in 1939 in Nelson, BC. He grew up in the Kootenay and Okanagan regions of the BC Interior, primarily in Vernon. He came to Vancouver and co-founded a small press, Very Stone House, with bill bissett and Seymour Mayne. He then drifted extensively throughout North and South America. He has worked at a variety of jobs from labourer to industrial accountant, but much of his life has been spent as a poet, having produced twenty-four books of poetry to date. He is also the father of five children and grandfather of eleven. He is an Officer of The Order of Canada and has won nearly every literary prize in Canada, from the Governor General's Award to the Canadian Authors Association Award to the Dorothy Livesay Poetry Prize. His poetry and fiction have been widely anthologized and have been translated into many languages. Lane now makes his home in Victoria, BC, with his companion, the poet Lorna Crozier.